Novello Shakespeare
Choral Collection

edited by David Wordsworth

Published by
Novello Publishing Limited
14–15 Berners Street,
London W1T 3LJ, UK.

Exclusive Distributors:
Music Sales Limited
Distribution Centre, Newmarket Road,
Bury St Edmunds, Suffolk IP33 3YB, UK.

Music Sales Corporation
180 Madison Avenue, 24th Floor,
New York NY 10016, USA.

Music Sales Pty Limited
Level 4, Lisgar House,
30–32 Carrington Street,
Sydney, NSW 2000 Australia.

Order No. NOV164681
ISBN 978-1-78305-615-6

Edited by David Wordsworth.
Project managed and edited by Jonathan Wikeley.
Engraving by Paul and Julie Ewers.
Cover design by Ruth Keating.

Printed in the EU.

Contents

'If music be the food of love, play on...' wrote William Shakespeare in *Twelfth Night* — in this case 'sing on' might be more apt; songs played a major part in many of Shakespeare's plays, and songs, sonnets, poems and monologues have proved an irresistible source of inspiration for so many composers through the ages. The idea for this anthology stemmed from the 400th anniversary of the death of Shakespeare in 2016, and an invitation from the Shakespeare Birthplace Trust to direct 'Singing Shakespeare', a celebration of choral settings of the Bard. I am very grateful to the team at Novello for all their support, especially Jonathan Wikeley, Matthew Berry, and Paul and Julie Ewers.

The aim of the book is to provide as wide a variety of pieces as space allows, and to give choirs of all kinds and abilities the chance to present a concert programme that is at once fun to sing, occasionally challenging, and appealing to audiences. Many pieces, such as Thomas Arne's 'Blow, blow, thou winter wind', William Schuman's 'Orpheus with his lute' and Lennox Berkeley's 'Hymn for Shakespeare's Birthday' are easy to put together and rehearse, and show off their effectiveness in the most direct way; those that require a little more rehearsal will more than repay any time spent on them — Richard Sisson's 'Light Thickens' is a mischievous squint at the witches' scene in *Hamlet*, and Kevin Olson's 'A Summer Sonnet' is an infectious jazz number.

I am most grateful to the composers who readily agreed to write new pieces especially for this book. John Joubert — one of the most significant figures in British choral music for the past half-century — responded with a beautifully transparent setting of 'Be not afeared', while the incredibly versatile Richard Sisson was inspired to write his characteristically witty 'Light Thickens'. Paweł Łukaszewski has made an arrangement for SATB choir of his setting of Sonnet XXVII and we have had the great good fortune to publish for the first time contrasting and imaginative responses to Shakespeare texts by Kevin Olson, Bernard Hughes and John Gardner. In addition my thanks are due to Stephen Sondheim for generously agreeing to the inclusion of his wistful version of 'Fear no more'. My one regret is that my friend John McCabe was too ill to finish what promised to be a fascinating setting of a text from King Lear — I know how much he wanted to complete his piece and it touches me deeply to know that he even thought about doing so during the final stages of his terrible illness. This book is partly dedicated to this much missed and remarkable pianist and composer.

The man that hath no music in himself,
Nor is not mov'd with concord of sweet sounds,
Is fit for treasons, stratagems and spoils;

The motions of his spirit are dull as night,
And his afflictions dark as Erebus,
Let no such man be trusted.

David Wordsworth, July 2015

Notes on the music

Blow, blow, thou winter wind. *Thomas Arne (1710–78)* is now remembered as the composer of 'Rule Britannia' and the version of 'God Save the Queen' that became the British National Anthem. Arne was the most successful London theatre composer of his day; his works were staged at Drury Lane and Covent Garden. His setting of 'Blow, blow, thou winter wind' was originally a solo song and was more recently arranged for SATB choir by Desmond Ratcliffe.

Hymn to Shakespeare's Birthday *Lennox Berkeley (1903–89)*. Although not a text by Shakespeare, Berkeley's piece was commissioned by the actor Sam Wanamaker, then of the Globe Theatre Trust and the founding creative genius behind the revitalised Globe Theatre in London. The work sets a text by the then poet laureate Cecil Day Lewis (1904–72) and was first sung in Southwark Cathedral, to celebrate Shakespeare's birthday/death-day on April 23rd 1972.

Lo, here, the gentle lark *from* **The Food of Love Book I** *Gary Carpenter (1951–)*. This is the first song from *The Food of Love*: a series of choral songs with piano in four volumes for choirs of different dispositions (two for mixed voices, one for tenors and basses, one for sopranos and altos). The works were commissioned by the Shakespeare Birthplace Trust to commemorate the 400th anniversary of the death of Shakespeare and for 'Singing Shakespeare', a two-year project that encourages the performance and composition of choral settings of Shakespeare. Gary Carpenter has written operas and musicals, was music director for many films including *The Wicker Man* and has composed a large amount of concert music including a new work for the First Night of the Proms, 2015.

O, how much more *from* **Three Rose Madrigals** *Paul Crabtree (1960–)*. Born in the UK but long resident in the US, choral music is central to the output of Paul Crabtree. His works are inspired by subjects and texts as diverse as *The Simpsons*, Bob Dylan and Ted Hughes, and have been championed by the BBC Singers and The Cardinall's Musick among many others. 'O, how much more' is the first of three short pieces that set sonnets mentioning the word rose. They were written for the composer's aunt and uncle, in whose garden Crabtree explains he 'came to grips with the behaviour and idiosyncratic care of roses'.

Four Rounds to Shakespeare Texts *John Gardner (1917–2011)*. Written for the 1976 European Cantat, these four short pieces are further demonstration of Gardner's natural response to the setting of texts. Quirky, witty, but never unmusical, Gardner's teaching career at the Royal Academy of Music, St Paul's Girls' School and Morley College ensured that his approach was never less than practical. He is best remembered for two Christtmas carols — 'The holly and the Ivy' and in particular 'Tomorrow shall be my dancing day', but his varied choral output surely deserves revival.

Tell me where is fancy bred *from* **Shakespeare Songs Book II**
It was a lover and his lass *from* **Shakespeare Songs Book III**
Who is Silvia? *from* **Shakespeare Songs Book I** *Matthew Harris (1956–)*. The American composer Matthew Harris has frequently set texts by a wide range of British writers — Robert Burns, William Blake, Wendy Cope, Thomas Hardy, Dylan Thomas, William Wordsworth and most particularly William Shakespeare, who has inspired no fewer than six books of songs for unaccompanied chorus. These increasingly popular and attractive settings show the influence of the English madrigalists, the Broadway stage and American folksong.

Rosemary. *Daniel Helldén (1917–98)* was a Swedish composer, conductor and educator. Helldén studied with Carl Orff and was responsible for the introduction of Orff's ideas in Scandinavia. Most of his large output is for choir and includes many works for young performers.

If we shadows have offended *from* **A Midsummer Night's Dream**. *Bernard Hughes (1974–)* has described this incidental music as his first 'break' as a composer. Originally written as solo songs for a school production when he was 14, years later Hughes returned to the songs and arranged them for SATB chorus. Bernard Hughes is composer-in-residence at St Paul's Girls' School in London; his choral music has been sung by the BBC Singers, the Crouch End Festival Chorus and at the Three Choirs Festival.

Be Not Afeard *John Joubert (1927–)*. South African-born John Joubert has had a long and distinguished career as a teacher (at the universities of Hull and Birmingham) and composer. His choral works range from short carols and anthems, which have entered the regular repertoire of choirs the world over, such as 'Torches' and 'There is no rose', to large-scale choral and orchestral pieces, including 'An English Requiem', premiered to great acclaim at the 2010 Three Choirs Festival.

Shall I compare thee to a summer's day? *from* **A Lover's Journey** *Libby Larsen (1950–).*
Libby Larsen is one of America's most performed living composers with a wide-ranging
catalogue of over 500 works in every genre, including several operas and many choral
works. *A Lover's Journey* is a set of four pieces that tell what the composer describes as the
'elegant story of love and valentining'. Larsen presents *A Lover's Journey* as her 'Valentine
to the King's Singers', who commissioned the work.

How sweet the moonlight sleeps *Henry Leslie (1822–96).* A now forgotten figure in
British music, Leslie was the founding director of several large choral societies and a number
of national music schools, including the forerunner of the Royal College of Music in London.
His charming setting of words from *The Merchant of Venice* sets the text chosen by Vaughan
Williams for perhaps one of the most famous of all Shakespeare settings, 'Serenade to Music'.

Weary with toil, I haste me to my bed *Paweł Łukaszewski (1968–).* One of the relatively
few secular choral works by this acclaimed Polish composer, this piece was originally written
for the proMODERN contemporary vocal sextet and is arranged for SATB by the composer
for this anthology. Paweł Łukaszewski is Professor of Composition at the Frederyk Chopin
University in Warsaw and Artistic Director of Musica Sacra, Warsaw.

Ophelia's Lament *from* **Let Fall the Windows of Mine Eyes** *Paul Mealor (1975–).*
This, the first of three Shakespeare settings on the themes of remembrance and loss was
commissioned by the Voices of Shakespeare Festival in 2008 and sets part of Ophelia's
tragic lament over her father's death in *Hamlet*. Paul Mealor is Professor of Music at the
University of Aberdeen.

Sigh no more, ladies *Ernest Moeran (1894–1950).* Although born in west London, Moeran
had strong connections with Ireland whose traditional music and landscape inspired a good
deal of his work. Moeran's output includes several large-scale works including a symphony
and a violin concerto, but he often spoke of himself as being essentially a 'madrigalist', and
the influence of the English madrigalists and folk-song, and the jazz world of 1920s London,
can be heard in this delightful miniature.

A Summer Sonnet *Kevin Olson (1971–).* This work was written for an all-Shakespeare
concert given by Chicago a cappella. The ensemble encouraged composers to work in
differing styles, which lead Olson's discovery that the 14 lines of the sonnet worked within
the typical ABA form of jazz tunes. A jazz pianist himself, Olson transferred piano voicings

to the vocal lines, to capture what he calls 'the smooth, laid-back feel of the music of Antonio Carlos Jobim and other Latin masters'. Kevin Olson is a pianist, composer and a member of the piano faculty at Utah State University.

Orpheus with his lute. *William Schuman (1910–92)* began his musical career as the leader of a dance band 'Billy Schuman and his Alamo Society Orchestra' and rose to become President of both the Juilliard School and the Lincoln Center. Schuman was also the composer of an impressive series of ten symphonies, as well as many other orchestral and chamber works. Less well known is his extensive catalogue of choral pieces, of which this setting of 'Orpheus with his lute' is a beautiful and simple example. Schuman later used the song as the basis of his Cello Concerto 'A Song of Orpheus'.

Light Thickens *Richard Sisson (1957–)*. For many years one half of the double-act 'Kit and the Widow', Richard Sisson is also a distinguished composer of music for both the concert hall and the stage, enjoying a particularly close association with Alan Bennett, and writing incidental music for *The History Boys* and *The Lady in the Van*. He says of his piece, which was written for this collection: ''Light Thickens', is, I hope, an opportunity for a choir to luxuriate in the beauty of their most exquisite blend. Meanwhile, a devoted accompanist can spin a lyrical line above these softest of harmonies, while three of the naughtiest members of the choir-tap into their inner witch — like hell-broth boil and bubble!'

Fear no more *from* **The Frogs** *Stephen Sondheim (1930–) arr. David Wordsworth*. Stephen Sondheim and Burt Shevelove's adaptation of the Greek tragedy by Aristophanes follows the attempts of Dionysius, weary of living playwrights, who travels to Hades to bring back George Bernard Shaw and William Shakespeare to take part in a competition to find the best dramatist. 'Fear no more' appears as a solo song in Act II and results in the Bard winning the competition and being crowned the world's greatest playwright.

Fear no more *John Tavener (1944–2013)*. One of the most celebrated British composers of the late-20th and early-21st century, most of Tavener's music was a response to his deep religious faith and to sacred texts. He turned to Shakespeare later in his compositional career: 'Fear no more' was first sung in Salisbury Cathedral in May 2007 as part of a Requiem Mass for the Rev. Gerald Squarey, a close friend of the composer, who wrote: 'This work should be performed with ecstatic solemnity. It is as though the slowly shifting chords are a resonance from Eternity. The supreme Sanskrit syllable of OM at the end represents the

Infinite: after a bell-like attack, 30 seconds of humming should gently resonate around the building in calm contemplation.'

Look in thy glass *from* **Three Shakespeare Sonnets** *John Tavener (1944–2013)*. This piece was commissioned by the Ministry of Education and Culture in Iceland and first performed by the dedicatees, the South Iceland Chamber Choir at Southwark Cathedral, London, just a matter of days after the composer's death. Tavener wrote: 'The set of *Three Shakespeare Sonnets* was one of the first works that I composed after a serious illness in 2007. I wanted to pay tribute to my wife Maryanna, who nursed me back to some degree of health, so I turned to Shakespeare's sonnets. I was delighted to find that they brought forth music once again, after I had been silent for so long'.

Orpheus *from* **A Song Sung True** *Judith Weir (1954–)*. Judith Weir is composer-in-residence with the BBC Singers and the Master of the Queen's Music; 'Orpheus' is the second movement of her four-movement choral cycle *The Song Sung True*. Commissioned from a bequest of the late Helen Sibthorp, a member of the London Lawyers' Chorus, which gave the first performance, the texts for all of the pieces are concerned with music and singing.

Daffodils and **O mistress mine** *from* **A Shakespeare Suite** *Nancy Wertsch (1943–)*. Winner of the first prize in the Athena Festival of Women and Music in 2003 and premiered by the New York Virtuoso Singers, These two Shakespeare sonnets, taken from a set of three, were chosen by Wertsch to reflect youth, love and Spring. Nancy Wertsch is an experienced singer and composer, and lives in New York.

Full fathom five *Charles Wood (1866–1926)*. This Irish composer and teacher who numbered Vaughan Williams and Howells among his pupils is now chiefly remembered for his Anglican church music, but his output included a number of operas, a piano concerto, six string quartets and a large number of secular choral works.

Blow, blow, thou winter wind

As You Like It II:vii

Thomas Arne
(1710–78)
arr. Desmond Ratcliffe

Arranged from the version 'Sung by Mrs Clive' (1750?) and the Harrison Score of 1785(?).
The octaves in bars 18 and 40 are Arne's. *D. R.*

thou the wat - ers warp,_____ Thy sting__ is__ not__ so__ sharp__ As__

thou the wat - ers warp, Thy sting is not so sharp, so

thou_____ the wat - ers warp, Thy sting is not so sharp__ As

thou the wat - ers warp, Thy sting is not so sharp As

friend__ re - mem - bered__ not,_____ As friend re - mem-bered not,__ Thy

sharp As friend, as friend re - mem - bered not,__ Thy

friend re - mem - bered not,_____ As friend re - mem-bered not, Thy

friend re - mem - bered not,_____ Thy__

Hymn for Shakespeare's Birthday

Cecil Day-Lewis
(1904–72)

Lennox Berkeley
(1903–89)

fire. Af - ter that fie - ry___ birth___ What

end - less ae - ons throng Be - fore this___ green and

trou-bled earth Can___ grow to___ her full song!

cantabile

Commissioned by the Shakespeare Birthplace Trust

Lo, here, the gentle lark

from *The Food of Love Book I*

Venus and Adonis

Gary Carpenter
(b. 1951)

for Jenny and Graham Cousins

O, how much more

from *Three Rose Madrigals*

Sonnet 54

Paul Crabtree
(b. 1960)

28

Four Rounds to Shakespeare Texts

John Gardner
(1917–2011)

1. If music be the food of love

Twelfth Night I:i

Op. 133, No. 1

Composer's note:

This can be given in many ways: for instance the two rounds can be expounded separately then together; or it can be done as a single six-part round with the substitution of the E at the end of stave 3 by the A in brackets and by the omission of the final A of stave 6 where of course it is necessary to return to the top. Best way might be S. A. S. B. T. B. at two-bar intervals with S. S. T. on Round I and A. B. B. on Round II.

In this case do the given last bar.

The square fermata indicates the stopping point.

2. The Fool Speaks

Twelfth Night IV:ii

Op. 133, No. 2

Scherzando e presto possibile

Composer's note:

Better on equal voices (men's).

3. Under the greenwood tree

As You Like It II:v   Op. 133, No. 3

Composer's note:

Better on equal than on mixed voices and can be given by five (but not fewer) voices.

If liked, the voices can finish one by one rather than all together at the fermata.

4. Blow, blow, thou winter wind

As You Like It II:vii   Op. 133, No. 4

Composer's note:

If done by mixed voices, enter in the order A. S. B. T. and finish with the basses on the low A in stave 2.

It was a lover and his lass

from *Shakespeare Songs Book III*

As You Like It V:iii

Matthew Harris
(b. 1956)

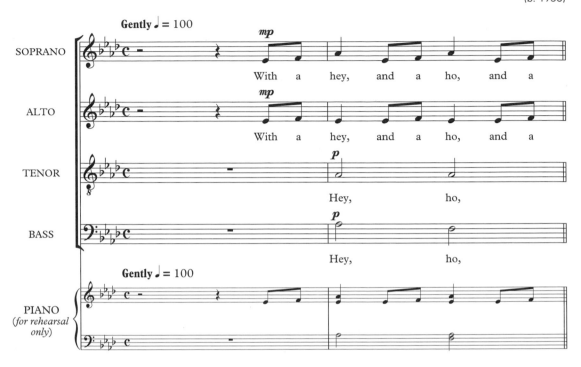

42

Tell me where is fancy bred

from *Shakespeare Songs Book II*

The Merchant of Venice III:ii

Matthew Harris
(b. 1956)

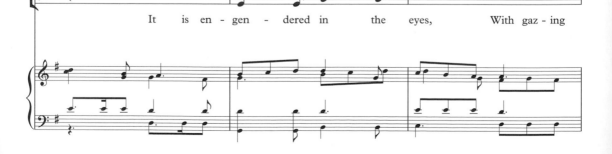

In— the cra-dle where it lies, in— the cra-dle where— it lies.

dies In— the cra-dle where it lies, in— the cra-dle where— it

and fan-cy dies In— the cra-dle where it lies, in— the cra-dle,

fed; and fan-cy dies In— the cra-dle where it lies.—

Let us all ring fan-cy's knell: I'll be-gin it— Ding, dong, bell,

lies. Let us all ring, let us all ring, let us all ring,—

Ding, dong, bell, let us

Let us all ring, let us all ring, let us all ring, let us all ring,

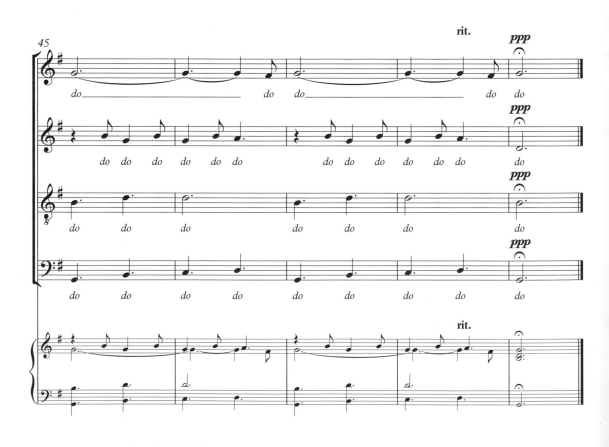

Who is Silvia?

from *Shakespeare Songs Book I*

Two Gentlemen of Verona II:iv

Matthew Harris
(b. 1956)

* Solo Tenor sings at pitch.

Rosemary

Hamlet IV:v

Daniel Helldén
(1917–98)

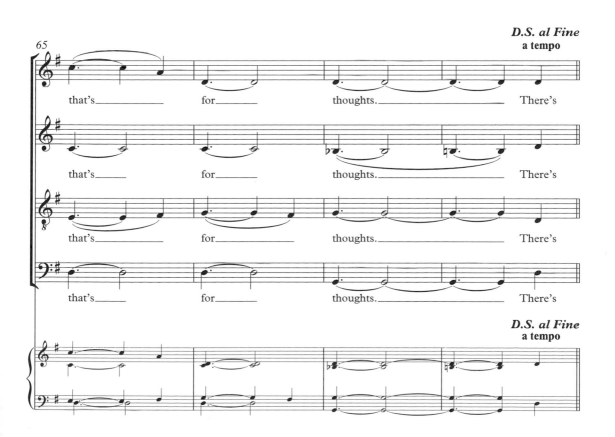

If we shadows have offended

from *A Midsummer Night's Dream*

A Midsummer Night's Dream V:i

Bernard Hughes
(b. 1974)

While these vi-sions did ap-pear. ah_____

While these vi-sions did ap-pear. ah_____

While these vi-sions did ap-pear. ah_____

While these vi-sions did ap-pear. And this weak and i-dle

ah_____ ah_____

ah_____ ah_____

ah_____ ah_____

theme, No more yield-ing but a dream, Gent-les, do not rep-re-

Give me your hands, if we be friends, And Ro-bin shall re-store a-

Give me your hands, if we be friends, And Ro-bin shall re-store a-

Give me your hands, if we be friends, And Ro-bin shall re-store a-

Give me your hands, if we be friends, And Ro-bin shall re-store a-

-mends, and Ro-bin shall re-store a-mends.

-mends, and Ro-bin shall re-store a-mends.

-mends, and Ro-bin shall re-store a-mends.

-mends, and Ro-bin shall re-store a-mends.

Commissioned by Music Sales to commemorate the
400th anniversary of Shakespeare's death.

Be not afeard

The Tempest III:ii

John Joubert
(b. 1927)

74

Shall I compare thee to a summer's day?

from *A Lover's Journey*

Sonnet 18

Libby Larsen
(b. 1950)

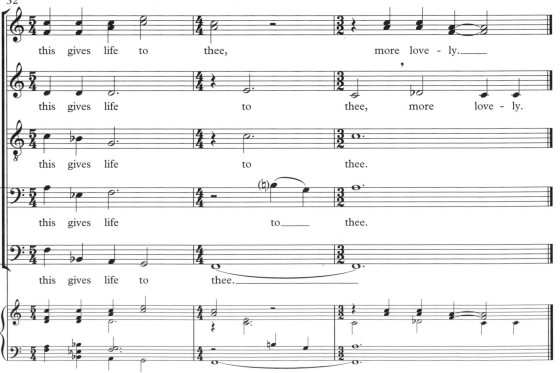

How sweet the moonlight sleeps

The Merchant of Venice V:i

Henry Leslie
(1822–96)

Weary with toil, I haste me to my bed

Sonnet 27

Paweł Łukaszewski
(b. 1968)

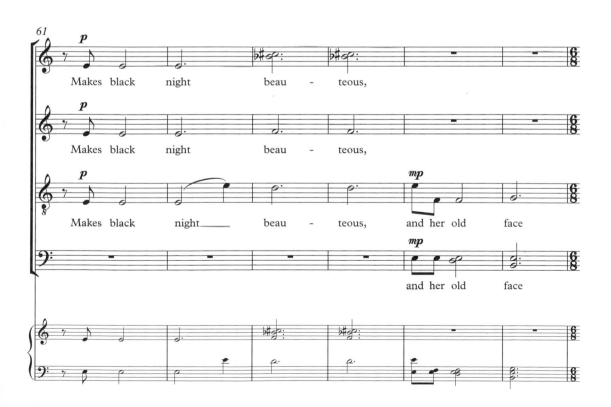

Ophelia's Lament

No. 1 from *Let Fall the Windows of Mine Eyes*

Hamlet IV:v

Paul Mealor
(b. 1975)

Sigh no more, ladies

Much Ado About Nothing II:iii

Ernest Moeran
(1894–1950)

100

A Summer Sonnet

Sonnet 18

Kevin Olson
(b. 1971)

108

118

124

Orpheus with his lute

Henry VIII III:i

William Schuman
(1910–92)

Light Thickens

Macbeth III:ii & II:ii

Richard Sisson
(b. 1957)

* Some altos with comfortable higher tessitura could be diverted to support the sopranos in these passages.

138

*The bent claw of a finger starts to tap at the window;
soon there are three of them tapping.
Louder and louder – now knocking at the door itself...

*The tapping starts very discreetly, perhaps even with scratching...

*We hear the whispered spells of the three cackling hags...
Muttering soullessly - each of them dancing to a different drum.

Fillet of a fenny snake,   Eye of newt, and toe of frog,   Adder's fork, and blind-worm's sting,   For a charm of powerful trouble,
In the cauldron, boil and bake;   Wool of bat, and tongue of dog,   Lizard's leg, and howlet's wing,   Like a hell-broth boil and bubble.

Tempo I ♩ = 72

breathy expiration...

While

Tempo I ♩ = 72

* (Each hag chants in a different rhythm and tempo - 4/4, compound duple and free-form perhaps)

* (The hags, at three different speeds, chant one complete word per beat)

Fear no more

from *The Frogs*

Cymbeline IV:ii

Stephen Sondheim
(b. 1930)
arr. David Wordsworth

* Stagger breath until bar 19

Fear no more

Cymbeline IV:ii

John Tavener
(1944–2013)

Thou thy world-ly task hast done. Home art gone, and
Thou thy world-ly task hast done. Home art gone, and
Thou thy world-ly task hast done. Home art gone, and
Thou thy world-ly task hast done. Home art gone, and

ta'en thy wa - ges. Al - le - lou - i - a,
ta'en thy wa - ges. Al - le - lou - i - a,
ta'en thy wa - ges. Al - le - lou - i - a,
ta'en thy wa - ges. Al - le - lou - i - a,

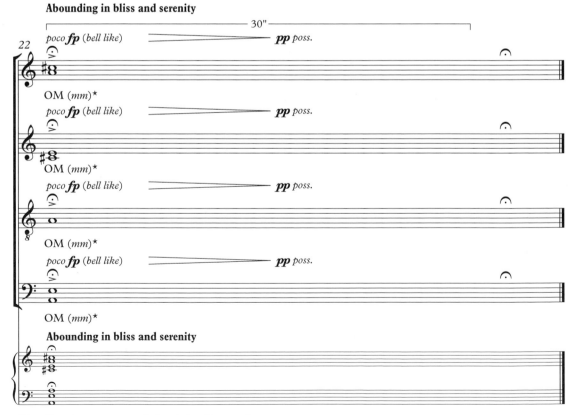

*Breathe when necessary, but not simultaneously.

Look in thy glass

from *Three Shakespeare Sonnets*

Sonnet 3

John Tavener
(1944–2013)

Orpheus

from *A Song Sung True*

Henry VIII III:i

Judith Weir
(b. 1954)

Daffodils

from *A Shakespeare Suite*

The Winter's Tale IV:ii

Nancy Wertsch
(b. 1943)

* doxy - *mistress*

* Close to "mm" immediately.

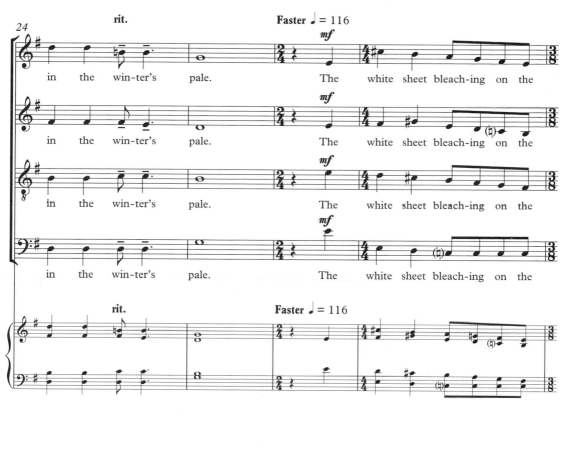

* pugging - *thieving*

* aunts - *sweethearts*

First prize, Ithaca College Choral Composition Competition, 1997

O mistress mine

from *A Shakespeare Suite*

Twelfth Night II:iii

Nancy Wertsch
(b. 1943)

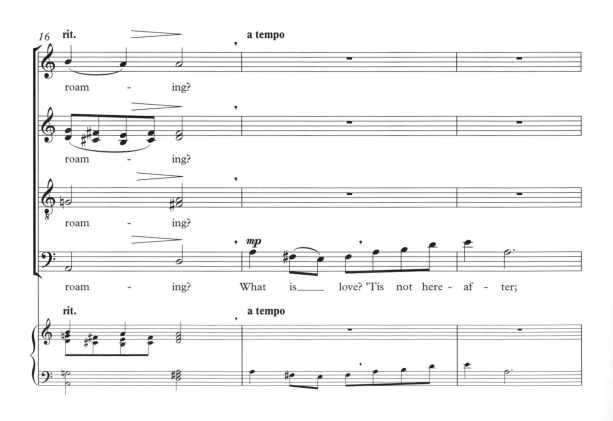

Full fathom five

The Tempest I:ii

Charles Wood
(1866–1926)

Now available

THE NOVELLO BOOK *of*
BRITISH
FOLKSONGS

For mixed-voice choirs

With an introduction by Jeremy Summerly

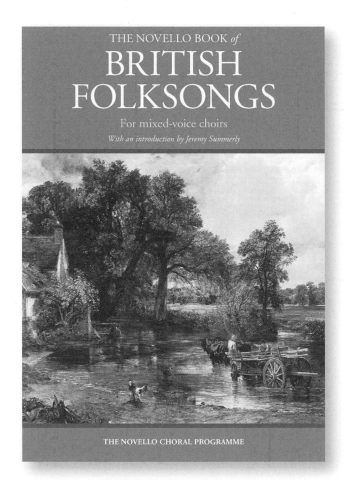

Order No. NOV164450

FRENCH SONGS & CHORUSES

for mixed-voice choir

French songs and choruses for choirs is a collection of some of the finest original choral music by French composers, and delightful arrangements of some of the greatest and most beautiful French songs. The volume is suitable for choirs of all sizes and abilities, and makes for a fine concert programme in itself, as well as being an inviting treasure trove of pieces to dip into.

Order No.: NOV165198